In Silence with Mohanji

IN SILENCE WITH MOHANJI

Precious Moments of Connection

LINDA ABROL

Gurulight

In Silence with Mohanji—Precious Moments of Connection
By Linda Abrol

Acknowledgements and Credits:
Cover image: Tea Klincov
Cover design: Prashanti Abrol
Editor: Rajesh Kamath

1st Edition: June 2022

Published by Gurulight
Email: info@gurulight.com
Website: www.gurulight.com

Disclaimer:

The views, opinions and positions expressed in this book by the author on these testimonials are mine alone. They do not necessarily reflect the views, opinions or positions of Mohanji, Mohanji Foundation, its members, employees or any other individual or entity associated with Mohanji or Mohanji Foundation. I make no representations of the accuracy, completeness, timeliness, suitability or validity of any information presented and will not be liable for any errors, omissions, or delays in this information or any losses, injuries or damages arising from its display or use.

Linda Abrol

DEDICATION

I dedicate this book in heartfelt gratitude
to my beloved friend, spiritual guide, brother, and
Guru—Parabrahma Mohanji.

My Guruswamy, Shri Sathya Sai Baba,
Swami Shri Gopal Baba, Father, Dattatreya, Jesus,
Krishna, Buddha; all in One and beyond

He is SUPREME SILENCE

May this book be an inspiration to all those who are willing to dive deep into the Hall of Silence in their heart to find precious moments of connection with the Eternal Beloved

Yogiraj, Parabrahma, Shri Sacchidananda Sadguru,
Mohanji Maharaj ki Jai!

ONENESS

"YOU MADE MY day, Linda!" was my response to Linda's message that she was compiling a book of her experiences with Mohanji. Pleasantly surprised by the excitement in my voice, she became emotional herself! I explained the reason for my excitement.

On the auspicious day of Shirdi Sai Baba's hundredth Mahasamadhi[1], I received this guidance, "Over five hundred Mohanji testimonials are spread out on various blogs. It's high time that Mohanji Satcharita[2] is available for people. A book of real experiences that will channel the energy of pure consciousness through the followers' connection with the Master. Each word in this book will not just narrate the Truth but also be a pearl of pure energy. One will feel an immediate connection to Mohanji's consciousness just by holding the book. That will be the power of the Mohanji Satcharita."

I had been publishing the testimonials on the various blogs but had not thought of publishing a book! This guidance woke me up! Soon I reached out to Mohanji for His permission. I knew this wasn't a random thought but Divine guidance from the Tradition. Mohanji kindly permitted us, and the team soon geared up to collect stories for the book.

Without knowing the basics of publication, we jumped headfirst into the task of publishing this book. We put the *sankalpam* (intention) and were determined to deliver. On 1st January 2019, I met Mohanji at his Palakkad home and mentioned the book. Mohanji gave me clear, practical instructions in his usual style and even connected me to the right people. Three weeks after this discussion, 'Guru Leela', the first Mohanji Satcharita, was in Mohanji's hands during our Acharya Training in Bangalore on 21st January 2019.

Our host for the Acharya training, Mr Subramanian, a sincere follower of Sathya Sai Baba and Mohanji, almost went into a trance when he held the book. He uttered, "Just by holding this book, I feel the immense grace of the entire Guru Mandala. This book is not ordinary; it will transform people's lives as Mohanji's pure energy is embedded in it." I was speechless to hear the exact words I had received in my guidance! I took them as a confirmation coming from the higher Masters!

I realised then the power that worked behind making the book 'Guru Leela' a reality. Neither our expertise nor our capacity mattered! The Tradition was behind it! This was a true eye-opener to all of us—the importance of experience sharing. Mohnaji says, "Testimonials are how the Tradition reveals its presence. When you honestly write your experiences, it becomes a service to the Tradition."

From 'Guru Leela 1 in January 2019 to 'Guru Leela 5' in February 2022, the journey has been personally rewarding for me and the team working wholeheartedly behind it. It has been our greatest sadhana (spiritual practice) and seva (selfless service) to Mohanji and through Him to the Masters of the Tradition. Hence, Linda's book was ecstatic news for me!

I have known Linda since August 2021. I met her at the Consciousness Kriya training specially conducted during Mohanji's first visit to the Netherlands. I had a beautiful and instant bonding with this group. I have been very blessed to read and listen to her experiences shared consistently and continuously through the months of the fast-track journey of her connection with Mohanji. I also witnessed her journey through the Mai-Tri and MTM[3] sessions for her. I have seen her growing connection, elimination of doubts, stronger conviction and clarity of purpose!

I am sure that the readers will feel the purity and intensity of her connection to Mohanji. The essence of this book is Oneness! You will realise that when you read this book till the very end and feel this essence oozing from every word!

My heartiest CONGRATULATIONS to Linda for bringing this book to life. I sincerely thank her for allowing me to share my thoughts.

Happy Reading.
Lots of Love,
Subhasree Thottungal

3 Mai-Tri and Mohanji Transformation Method (MTM) are profound methods for deep cleansing and harmonising using Mohanji's energy.

FOREWORD

LINDA HAS BEEN my friend for many years. We have shared some deep fond memories with Swami Gopal Baba and even written a book about him. Linda is very sensitive to subtle energies and has received profound messages from the Supreme Soul for more than thirty years. When we were told, just a few days in advance, that Mohanji would come to the Netherlands in August 2021, I was sure that she would be one of the people who would be willing to help me with the preparations.

Since then, it has been so beautiful to see her love for Mohanji grow and blossom. Soon, she received his sweet messages in her heart. It takes a lot of courage to share what is so tender and precious for oneself with the world. I am grateful that she did because I felt that reading this book encourages us to value and cherish our experiences.

God speaks to all of us, but do we listen? Thank you, Linda, for setting an example. Please keep sharing.

With gratitude and love,
Sita van den Nieuwendijk

ACKNOWLEDGEMENT

I WOULD LOVE TO express my heartfelt gratitude to Mohanji and Subhasree. They believed in me and supported this small contribution of my personal experience with one of Mohanji's core teachings—*finding the Master within through silence.*

My gratitude goes out to my daughter, Prashanti. She has the gift of making covers and flyers that depict their exact purpose.

And many, many thanks to all the hardworking volunteers who facilitate the book printing process within the Mohanji Foundation.

Through this book, I do not intend to influence, encourage or reorient the reader in any particular direction. My wish mirrors Mohanji's view on testimonials—to make readers appreciate and value their experiences, as writing this book made me value mine. Otherwise, we tend to forget even the best of our experiences when the mind takes over.

MOHANJI ON FINDING THE MASTER WITHIN[4]

THERE IS A Master inside all of us. The true education or true teaching is to bring that Master out. This Master is simply quiet, silent inside us. We all have a Master inside, our true Master.

In Sanskrit, it's called atma tattva, which means soul factor. We have a soul inside, that is the energy, which is stable and running just like electricity, which is going through all the gadgets.

How can you find the soul factor?

Through silence. When you become silent; when you start accepting yourself, respecting yourself, loving yourself, connecting with yourself continuously for a period of time, then you start feeling the energy moving inside you. You can use Kriya, you can use meditation, you can use anything, you have so many methods. But the main thing is you are consistent. It's about you.

4 Source: The Power of Purity by Mohanji (published with permission from Gurulight. All copyrights for this text belong to their respective owners)

PREFACE

How do you begin to write a book about silence? I would rather leave this page blank than write words we cannot taste. Words are just the mind's tasteless creations, where all we can taste is ourselves. What we usually do, say, experience or even read is what we are not. It is mostly about our thoughts and feelings about possessions, positions, and relationships that bind us to illusion levels. Only beyond my busy mind's smells, tastes, sights, and feelings have I experienced myself as purity and wholeness in moments of precious connection with the Master's energy.

So much has happened for me since Mohanji came to the Netherlands in August 2021! A state of flux that allowed unexpected and hidden parts of my personality to come up to dissolve the woes in Mohanji's presence and give me self-confidence and empowerment to participate in the many uplifting activities for Mohanji Netherlands Foundation.

He touched me deeply from the first meeting on all levels of conscious existence. I spontaneously and naturally allowed him to as if it had always been and was supposed to be so. Through my inner permission, I began to have inner experiences that were sensational and often direct guidance. There is no direct connection to the Master other than being in His energy. The guidance I received through inner words from this connection in silence felt true and complete. No noise. Often a direct confirmation of my inner experience came through a statement from Mohanji during an online meeting like the Empowerment workshops[5] or through other mediums.

I wrote down and shared each experience with the Testimonial Team or on various platforms of the Mohanji Foundation. Though with hesitation lest my repeated sharings annoy people. But not doing something out of fear is also ego; it binds. I wanted to overcome that fear because I love freedom. Encouraged by Mohanji's guidance on the benefits of experience sharing, I gathered all my courage and shared my experiences.

I compiled these sharings into this beautiful book. May the words bring flavour to the readers' hearts and be an inspiration to explore their inner state, raising their energy level to a higher frequency. May we become distinguish between the clutter and the permanent.

Love and Light,
Linda Abrol,
The Netherlands,
23rd May 2022

5 The Empowered workshop series was personally designed and delivered by Mohanji to allow people to move from fear to freedom and realise their true potential.

FROM THE TOP OF THE HILL 🦁

Be bold. Be brave. Own your experiences, and do not be afraid to say them out loud from the top of the hill. Even if the whole world ridicules you, do not be perturbed. Your experience is your own. There is no need for other people's acceptance.

~ Mohanji

CONTENTS

MEETING WITH THE MASTER

My story started with a telephone call from my dear friend and spiritual sister Sita, "Yesterday, I heard Mohanji is coming to the Netherlands! Not in six months, but in six days! I have been asked to organise *satsangs* (spiritual discourses) in various locations, a Fruit Tree Plantation Drive, and many other events. Would you like to help me?' I promised to help her organise Mohanji's first-ever official welcome in Holland. I knew nothing about Mohanji, barring a few pictures of his meeting with our spiritual Master, Swami Prabbhudananda Saraswati Maharaj (Swami Shri Gopal Baba), who took samadhi in July 2020.

In 1991, I was blessed to meet my beloved Shri Sathya Sai Baba (hereafter referred to as Sathya Sai), who I believed to be God's embodiment on earth. My visit to His ashram in Puttaparthi felt like I had finally come home. During the same journey to India, I met my first spiritual teacher, Guruswamy from Ponnampet, who was closely connected to Sathya Sai. Their unity in the spirit was clear to me because Sathya Sai appeared in the form of Guruswamy, whom I didn't know at the time, in a dream in 1990. When I saw Guruswamy physically in 1991, I recognised Him from my dream and was attracted to Him like a magnet. His words were like fragrant blossoms for my yearning heart.

Ten years later, Guruswamy passed away, and I was

inconsolable. But I had the amazing good fortune to be guided by the same Divine Force in another body, Swami Gopal Baba (hereafter referred to as Swami) from Girinagar. He had promised to rescue us, the followers, from the sea of *samsara* (the mundane cycle of birth and death) and lay us safely on Sathya Sai's lap. Swami visited our house, where we had our small Shri Sai Mandiram, in the South of Holland. Eighteen years since that day, he had stayed with us thrice. During those years, we facilitated monthly *satsangs* and weekly *abhishekam* (ritual bathing) of the *lingam*[6] materialised by Swami in 1991, which he named Vaidyanatheshwara (the Divine Doctor). Swami never told us about the lingam. We read it in a book called *Sai Darshan*, written by B.R. Ananthasayana Rao, a few years after its materialisation.

After Swami took samadhi in June 2020, I felt incredibly sad. Though I realised that the inner Guru, the divine memories and His *samadhi*[7] *mandir* (temple) in India were His legacies, there was a feeling of abandonment. "Why did Swami leave us in such difficult times? He did not even fulfil His promise to lay us in Sathya Sai's lap. We are far from God-realised.", I heard myself thinking more than once. Though I knew that my mind was luring me with limited thoughts, they felt like a reality to me. Trapped under these negative thoughts, loneliness engulfed my heart, making it difficult to raise my energy.

Sometimes, the sun shone through on hearing the sweet and soft inner voice that I have been blessed to hear since 1998 when

6 a statue that physically represents the infinite, formless aspect of Lord Shiva

7 Samadhi refers to both a saint's conscious exit from the body and his final resting place. In this context, it refers to the latter.

I was twenty-five years old. This voice has guided me more than anything from the outside world. Swami had acknowledged that this Divine voice was coming directly from the Source (God). This sweet, loving, inclusive, consoling, uplifting voice never forcefully directed me. Always a gentle nudge with ample room for contemplation and choice.

Since Swami's *samadhi*, I was not searching for a spiritual Master. I had no desire, feeling or intention to get close to yet another embodiment of Divinity since I thought that would only add to my confusion. Instead of one, I had already been close to three Divine Masters. Hence, I decided to meet Mohanji as my *bada Gurubhai* (my older spiritual brother). Also, I just wanted to help Sita. Having learnt that energy is contagious, I feel it is always beneficial to be near someone of a higher energy frequency. I was sure that Mohanji *bhai* (brother) had a super high, divine energy level.

The church of the Apostolic Society was the venue for Mohanji's *satsang*. I decorated the church with Sita's dear friend Loes. Having no idea about the content of Mohanji's *satsang* program, we were open and curious. When Mohanji arrived, He stepped out of the car, embraced Sita, walked right up to me and held me tight in a warm embrace, which He seemed to prolong for a while deliberately. In the picture taken of that memorable moment, I have such a bright smile that can only come from deep recognition, bliss and closeness. He touched my soul, and my heart opened spontaneously.

However, my mind chose to stay a little reserved and check things out first. This choice lasted fifteen minutes! Fifteen minutes was all it took to gain full faith in a spiritual Master! An absolute speed record, given that it took me years to adjust to the concept of having a guru after I first met Guruswamy in 1991. I was hugging a complete stranger with long hair, wearing jeans and a sweater. I fell for His Divine energy, His simple and understandable answers to our questions, His no-nonsense attitude, His detached warmth and compassion, and most of all, the feeling of inner recognition. It was as if my *bada* spiritual *bhai* (elder spiritual brother) had come, as if we had known each other forever, as if my God, my teachers and my Jesus had all come in one form. Even though He is a lion and I am only an ant in Consciousness, something opened in my Essence and met Him there—no resistance.

On my way to the next meeting in Onderdijk, I asked myself if I would be willing to do service for Mohanji's organisation as Sita had asked. I had served the Sai organisation in Holland for many years, followed by the service for Swami Gopal Baba's GKS family. I felt it would definitely cause a short circuit in my brain if I added the Mohanji family to the list. In between the car sounds and my busy thoughts, these words suddenly penetrated my awareness, "*When you regard me as your brother, would you refuse to do something for me if I asked you?* It was as though I heard Him speaking inside of me. Of course, that was the answer! Being one family, I would never refuse my elder brother any help.

That day, I could explain my (our) problem to Him and ask the question that bothered me most, "Mohanji bhai, how do we relate to You? We had the great fortune to have the Intimate and intense presence of Shri Sathya Sai Baba and Swami Prabbhudananda Saraswati Maharaj (Swami Gopal Baba) in our lives. Both have passed away. Connecting to yet another embodiment of Divinity feels like a betrayal to them.' Mohanji bhai explained that neither of them had actually passed away. They were continuing their mission. Being pure Consciousness, they were never confined to a body. They had always been and would always be just that—pure Consciousness.

I felt, "So is Mohanji." There is only one. There is no Mohanji. Just Consciousness. The same Consciousness. Although we had been mentally aware of this truth, it had somehow been hidden under the veil of our grief, loneliness and feelings of abandonment. Mohanji's words refreshed us with a more limitless viewpoint. After hearing these words, I noticed that my heart and the hearts of all those present opened like beautiful flowers on a bright and sunny day. We understood that our timeless and precious Swami had not abandoned us and instead kept his promise by sending Mohanji bhai to guide us further on our Journey to God.

Explaining further, Mohanji said, "If a family member—a mother, father, brother or sister—asks you to do something, would you refuse because you had already served another family member?' I was dumbstruck and delighted, for these words acknowledged what was conveyed to me in the car just an hour ago.

We asked questions closest to our hearts and listened endlessly to Mohanji's deep and resonating voice without getting tired or noticing our need for food or drink. Mohanji seemed entirely at ease amongst our relatively small group gathered at His feet in the Onderdijk Sai Temple. We wondered why a spiritual lion of His stature would come to a small town to spend so many hours with the few of us. One day, we sat with Him for eight hours or more! In an answer, Mohanji looked at the huge Sathya Sai picture on the altar and said that He could never refuse Sathya Sai's call.

After Mohanji left for Finland, I went to refresh the flowers on my father's grave, parking my car next to the Laurentius church where I went as a child. I felt a desire to write to Mohanji. I wrote to Him that I prayed to Jesus in this church as an innocent child, asking for a new bike. When I didn't get the bike, I figured that prayer didn't work. I wrote that I had finally met my Jesus (in Mohanji) but didn't need the bike anymore 😊. Let alone the bike, I needed nothing else from life. All that remained was longing for God-realisation. I wrote to Mohanji that I had complete faith that He would take his little sister's hand and guide her safely on this path, be the journey short or long.

Mohanji replied, "*Tathastu!* (So be it) *Tathastu! Tathastu*! May you always remain connected to my Consciousness. I am always with you and have always been in many forms. With love, Mohanji."

It warmed my heart, and I felt that this was a universal message. The realisation struck me that this is so true, so personal yet impersonal at the same time. Like Krishna, Mohanji bhai gave the heart a feeling of ultimate intimacy. Yet, He could never be personal without being universal at the same time. Like a gopi[8], I felt that He was there for me completely and totally, and I was aware that all the *gopis* must have had the same feeling. Not exclusive or inclusive, but a feeling of being exclusively close to one while including everyone.

8 Female companion of Lord Krishna. The male companions were called gopas.

WELCOME TO THE TRADITION OF DATTATREYA

Holiday time! The week following Mohanji's first Netherlands visit, I booked a campsite in our hometown neighbourhood. After a turbulent night, Mohanji's voice in the morning came as a pleasant surprise, "*Welcome to the Dattatreya Tradition*!" That sounded really special, even though I had to look up who or what Dattatreya was. I immediately asked in surprise, "Why the welcome to the Tradition? I have not even been initiated yet and am still a *Kriya*[9] baby!"

"*You are a Kriya Yogi now. You passed the first test*", was the immediate response. The previous night in the caravan, I was almost gassed by highly toxic sulfur dioxide. I smelt rotten eggs (the odour of sulfur dioxide), looked around, found nothing and tried to sleep. A little later, I got up again to do something I had forgotten and felt heat on the bench. In caravans, you have benches with lids under which you can store things. I opened the lid and found a red-hot battery with its contents bubbling out. I remembered seeing on the internet that a boiling battery should be removed immediately.

---

9 Kriya is a powerful ancient method of energy and breath control that enables a seeker to lead a life free from the mind's shackles and its patterns.

It was midnight. I looked out and was grateful to see a beer-drinking neighbour walking outside. I alerted him and requested help. He immediately came and removed the boiling battery from the caravan. Had the root cause remained unnoticed, I could have died slowly from inhaling toxic fumes or, worse, been seriously injured from a possible explosion. I remained calm the whole time through the crisis. That incident was the test!

One day later, Mohanji explained the situation with these inner words, "*Be a witness to everything. It is not that you are out of everything. It is that you resign everything.*" This episode happened before I had read any of Mohanji's books or participated in the Empowerment workshops. I practically knew nothing about him. Anyway, I passed the test successfully. We are not outside our experiences when we resign from them. We may experience pain, fear or problems, but we do not need to suffer. Suffering is mind.

"*No one has ever come to the Tradition who is not fully transformed.*" I was utterly perplexed by this inner message. Imagine the impact of these words. We are in safe hands and will reach our destination sooner or later. Failure is not an option! I wondered, "*How does this transformation happen?*" He answered, "*It starts with the transformation of the senses.*" I had no clue how the Tradition would transform the senses. Thus started the lessons for transformation, which later chapters shall reveal.

A FOOD STORY

Earlier, I had a daily habit of eating a sweet after dinner, despite knowing my body's difficulty processing it. This habit helped avoid suppression of my cravings for sweets which would have had an adverse effect. An effective compromise. An excellent first step that allowed me to enjoy the 'sinful' moment a lot! This habit reduced my craving, but the urge was easily evoked. After many years, I stopped this habit.

One day, Mohanji spoke to a lady about offering food to animals as a remedy to overcome food habits. That was permission enough to restart the habit. I allowed myself two cookies after dinner and fed some to the ducks. The cookies contained chocolate, gluten and sugar—three items that my body resists. I knew that ducks couldn't digest grains easily, but I gave it anyway since the crumbs were little. Mohanji's voice gently rebuked me the following morning, "*You didn't do me a favour.*" He said it humorously with a half-smile.

An incident that happened many years ago came to mind. In those days, I overate frequently. After I met Sathya Sai, I heard His voice inside me one morning saying, "*What did you eat? I ate aspirin yesterday.*" In two simple sentences, He made our unity very clear and ensured that I understood that the God part in me suffered from overeating due to the increased difficulty in raising my frequency to concentrate and meditate. Thus, conscious eating has great advantages on the spiritual path. I love that both Sathya Sai and Mohanji don't judge me like I often do. They gently make me aware of the consequences, which is very helpful. I love you, Mohanji! ♡♡♡

YOU WILL FORGET EVERYTHING ELSE

While I was sitting in my little temple one morning, the thought came, "Will I be as forgetful as my parents?" They both had Alzheimer's. Realising that my thoughts were not helping me, I let them pass. Suddenly I heard Mohanji say inwardly, "*I will give you so much love that you will forget everything else!*" What a beautiful message! Picking me up from where I was, He turned me into a whole new direction! My heart jumped, and my spirit elevated to bliss.

Subsequently, I went into my heart's cave while doing my practices and found Mohanji there. He embraced me and did not let me go. I could do nothing but cry. Totally in bliss, I forgot everything. The pain of the impending death of my dear mother vanished and turned into bliss, bliss, bliss. I loved being forgetful! How was this possible? How could I feel blissful when my dear mother, who was so close to me, was dying? I knew I would cry a lot in the coming days, but I was sure this would carry me through the process. ♡♡♡

GURU CONSCIOUSNESS

I would like to share a few short but important experiences from the last few days of the Empowerment 1 program and the days immediately after.

While walking with my little dog, a white-grey Maltezer Shitzu, I heard Mohanji's voice inside me saying, "*Guru Consciousness*". The Guru Consciousness is very important to me and all those who want to grow spiritually since the clutter creeps in its absence and takes over easily in this time of Kali Yuga[10].

Whenever I hear Mohanji's voice inside, I feel very connected and safe because connecting to Him is like losing boundaries and merging with consciousness. Later, Mohanji clearly explained the benefits of keeping one's awareness on the Guru during the workshop.

10 The fourth and worst of the four yugas (world ages) in Hinduism. It is believed to be the present age, full of conflict and sin.

CLOSE YOUR EYES

While practising Consciousness Kriya one day, suddenly these words resounded within me, "*Close your eyes.*" It was a strange suggestion considering that Kriya is practised with closed eyes. I then realised that I visualize during one of the exercises. I decided to forgo the visualization this time and stay purely with the feeling. The suggestion was to close my inner vision, which immediately deepened the experience. Mohanji's words during the Empowerment workshop, "Feel more and think less", came to mind. As I stayed with the feeling, white energy rose from my lower abdomen, continuing through my torso and skull to the space just above my head. The energy spread to the left and right like two huge arms or wings.

The sensation was upward and immense. Not only physically but on many levels. I felt as if I experienced a part of Christ Consciousness. I purposely say 'a part' because I believe there is no limit to the ever-expanding Christ Consciousness. The intensely compassionate and all-encompassing energy brought tears to my eyes. I decided not to focus on the emotion but to stay instead with the Christ feeling. I was drawn upwards, rose above myself and opened up. I felt as if an angel's energy was inside me, and I had disappeared for a moment. This energy had neither judgment nor fear—just intensity, warmth, compassion, love, and expansion.

Many weeks later, as I was pondering and trying to remember this experience, I felt the same white energy rise and spread above my head like wings. I heard Mohanji say, "These are the wings of the Tradition." I felt honoured and awed to have a tiny vision and experience of this mystical community called the Tradition that is so immense that we cannot fathom its extent and depth.

This state was not permanent but impressive enough to share because we forget our experiences when the mind takes over. Mohanji encourages us to share to acknowledge our experiences and empower ourselves. Jai Mohanji!

I AM THE FATHER OF FATHERS

One day, I had this beautiful experience, feeling Christ-Consciousness during Kriya. I didn't want to start the session with expectations, so I opened to '*whatever is here right now*'. I reminded myself to place my attention on feeling rather than visualising. Then I saw Jesus carry a lamb carefully and lovingly in His arms and place it on an altar (or platform). Symbolically, I felt that I was the lamb, totally safe in the arms of the Divine, and the altar represented my final destination—God. Words resounded as if from the heavens, "*I am the Father of Fathers.*" Although I had never thought of God as my father, I felt like I had come home.

One word spontaneously escaped with a sigh from my mouth, '*Mohanji*'. I wondered, "Where did that come from?" It was a call from deep within my soul, bubbling up from my very essence. Intense compassion. I cried tears of happiness and love. ♡ Again, I didn't stay with the emotion but instead went back to feeling as before. It was the Home of homes. Inexplainable.

When my thoughts started checking in, I heard myself asking, "Now what, Linda? You called Mohanji your bada bhai (elder brother), but your soul feels differently considering Him the Father of fathers (and of mothers, of course 😉)". Despite not being religious, this was the most sacred experience so far.

The following day, I was reading Mohanji's book, The Power of Purity, during lunchtime. He had gifted me this book in August 2021 when I had offered Him my book about Swami Gopal Baba, Grace and Wonder. I came across a picture of Jesus tenderly holding a lamb in His arms, to my utter astonishment. My cells started vibrating, and my heart skipped a beat on seeing this beautiful picture. It was a confirmation of my deeply touching and divine experience.

Jai Mohanji! ♡♡♡

NOTHING TO LOSE

It had been a while since I last wrote about my experiences. My mind was too occupied to slip into silence. We easily get distracted and lose ourselves in life's constant dramas. Some stories are dramatic and warrant our attention. My mother's recent terminal illness and passing away brought a lot of grief and sadness to our family. When the road gets rough, we forget to be the witness, which is human. Staying observant without judging myself and staying even-minded even while losing even-mindedness brings me back to balance.

Today, my Kriya experience was full of busy thoughts. After the online session, I tried to dive deeper into the silence since my silence had not been so silent. Somehow, I managed to relax, open up to love and let go, which resulted in a feeling of profound peace, and that was the moment I heard Mohanji's beloved voice say, *"How can you lose something here?*" In the peace, there was indeed nothing to lose or gain. Everything was there because nothing was there. Even the loss of my beloved mother faded into the background.

After the session, I again realised that all our activities were based on some form of fear. In silence, there is no fear. Hence there is nothing to lose. The mind is calm, so there is no faculty to create or remember fear. My heart opened, and a softness entered. A sweet 'beingness' that naturally passed into peace. I then heard inside: "Love is the closest step to peace".

Things somehow immediately fell into place. My experience of profound peace preceded by love demonstrated the truth of the above statement. All emotions are energy frequencies based primarily on fear of loss. Emotions range from low energy frequencies like anger and hatred to high energy frequencies like happiness, gratitude and love. I feel that love may be the highest energy the mind can experience before it surrenders to peace and subsides. Thus, love is always the most effective stepping stone to freedom.

Thank you, Sai Mohanji ♡

PROOF

At twenty-five (I am fifty-seven now), I had an identity crisis losing my partner, job, house, cat, friends and the very idea of who I was. One early morning during that time, I heard a voice, loud and intense, "*To the extent that the love for the Father of Fathers increases, the love for prosperity decreases.*"

At the time, I barely had a clue about its meaning. But it felt holy, intimate and deeply religious, like diving into my birth religion's essence—a reconnection, but on a completely different level. Two years later, I met Sathya Sai and somehow knew that He was the one guiding me towards the Light through the inner conversation. Mohanji explained how Sathya Sai, Swami and others had never died. They were pure consciousness and still are. The same consciousness came in the form of my beloved Father of Fathers, Mohanji.

While reading the Power of Purity, the following[11] on page 237 caught my immediate attention. "When the karmic attachment to material stuff diminishes, and attraction towards the subtle gets stronger, detachment towards worldly stuff takes root." Finally, in His no-nonsense style, I am getting the purest confirmation that He was the inner voice I started hearing when I was twenty-five years old!

11 Source: The Power of Purity by Mohanji (published with permission from Gurulight. All copyrights for this text belong to their respective owners)

STAY WITH ME

My mind can travel with a speed that deserves an ADHD diagnosis. Not that I have it, but anyway. Fortunately, it gets calm sometimes, for example, during some precious moments while practising Consciousness Kriya. Even while the mind is still active and jumping like a monkey, sometimes Mohanji's voice breaks through the storm like a calm breeze. Today, my mind was raising doubts about Mohanji liking me. I could imagine He would love me, but to like me personally is different.

Even though I felt totally and unconditionally connected during the first few weeks following our meeting in August this year, my monkey mind had decided that Mohanji would personally find me troublesome and annoying. Probably an old pattern of rejection surfaced. I even imagined Him talking to Chris and saying, "She will leave soon." When one feels scared and unloved, one tends to withdraw and protect oneself. One can't be the best and most lovely version of oneself in that mode. I witnessed this happening. Then I heard Mohanji's tender words inside, "*Stay with me.*"

I loved it and immediately felt accepted. I should never forget that the Guru never withdraws or leaves the disciple. *We* always do that due to negative beliefs about ourselves or past traumatic experiences.

While doing Consciousness Kriya Yoga one morning, I

wondered if it was necessary to hold *chin mudra*[12] all the time? I heard Mohanji's answer inside, "*The fingers represent the gunas*[13]." I was amazed. I was aware that the thumb and index finger represent universal consciousness (God) and individual consciousness. I wasn't aware of the meaning of the other three fingers. Curious as the mind is, I decided to look it up on the internet after the Kriya session. There it was, "The middle, ring and little finger symbolise the three gunas!"

Mohanji guided me so intimately and closely that I felt deeply moved.

Jai Sai Mohanji!

12 The hand pose of touching the tips of the thumb and index finger while keeping the other fingers straight.

13 One of three primal qualities or elements of matter according to Hindu philosophy

I AM THE BUDDHA

While doing my Kriya practice, my concentration was crisp and clear after I became the witness of my thoughts and concentrated on the stillness between the thoughts. I became the stillness. From that silence, the words emerged, "*I am beyond totality.*" followed by, "*I am the Buddha.*".

It was Mohanji speaking. I felt expanded and free—one with these statements. When asked to open my eyes, I didn't want to come out of silence. My mind started commenting afterwards: How can one be beyond totality when totality is everything? My being didn't doubt. It was just what it was—an experience. But a memorable one.

Jai Mohanji!

SCHOOL OF LIBERATION

In my previous writing, Mohanji told me in my Kriya meditation, "*I am beyond totality. I am the Buddha.*" Another inner statement, "*School of Liberation*", followed these words.

In our Shri Sai Mandiram home-temple inauguration, someone donated a beautiful Maitreya Buddha statue. I looked on the internet and found that Maitreya means Maitri (friendship) and that Maitreya will come to Earth, teaching liberation to the world! Hence, I thought, "Ah! A connection with Mohanji since Mai-Tri is Mohanji's healing method." I recalled the inner statement, "*I am the Buddha.*"

I was already aware that Mohanji's consciousness knows no boundaries. Now, I am awed to realise that He is the long-awaited Maitreya! Of course, amongst all the other Divine forms. Being my personal feeling, please don't dispute my words. Instead, name one deity whose incarnation He is not? 😊

THE SILENCE OF FOREVER

This Christmas, when I first saw a Facebook picture[14] of Mohanji seated in a deep inner, silent bliss with vibhuti (sacred ash) coming from His crown chakra and flowing over His face and shoulders, waves of bliss engulfed me, and tears flowed endlessly. I was looking at the personification of Shiva! Sai Shiva Mohanji! In the picture, I watched Him sitting with closed eyes in deep silence, merged with Sai Shiva consciousness, resembling a snowy mountain. I recalled some memories of the past.

When my mum was still alive[15], she had a small temple on the ceiling of my parental home where she practised her yoga and meditation. The temple had a drawing of Shiva meditating silently atop a mountain. Underneath were these words, "Sitting on the hill of my hopes in the glory of my enlightened consciousness." Many a time, I found myself repeating these words while I was meditating and visualising myself merged with this picture, sitting on the mountain top in the stillness and silence of the mighty mountain

14 From Mohanji's personal blog on His Shiva experience- https://brahmarishimohanji.wordpress.com/2010/07/28/babaji-beyond-definitions-part-3/

15 She passed away a few months before publishing this book

energy with Shiva's form and energy wrapped around and inside me.

I recalled one incident back as a small child in the classroom. The teacher was talking about the Himalayas. In the middle of his explanation, he asked us, "How would we feel being in the mountains?" When asked to speak, I immediately raised my arm and blurted out, "I would feel huge!" I meant that imagining myself amongst these mighty snowy mountains made me expand and become one with this energy. However, there was no chance to explain how I felt. The whole classroom burst out in laughter, for the expected answer was feeling tiny compared to these huge mountains. You can't explain some things, and people don't always understand what you mean. I never forgot the feeling of merging with the silent energy of the mountains.

One night, I woke up and saw four energy spots in a very engaging vision, one of which was supposed to have 'Shiva power'. I intuitively knew that I had to stand on each spot until I found the spot with Shankar Power. I did and received an energy jolt when I stepped on the last of the four spots. It was too much to bear, like being struck by lightning. As I screamed out to Sathya Sai for help, His huge face appeared next to me on the wall. I could see it, fully conscious with open eyes. It was no dream.

Years later, I found a picture of Sathya Sai's face but with Shiva's attributes—matted hair, third eye, snakes and the trident depicted next to Him. I love the picture as it became easier to see Sathya Sai as Shiva.

After the Kriya training, Mohanji spoke inside me, saying, "*The silence of forever.*" and sometime later, "*Enter this hall of silence. This is my gift to you.*" Shiva and Silence are one for me.

When I saw Mohanji's picture (mentioned earlier), I felt like I had come HOME. The feeling of coming home for Christmas was multiplied a thousand times. I feel the silent bliss every time I think of this picture.

When I do the Pause technique[16] and merge with the silence represented by this form, I see Him in my heart. I cannot help crying, knowing that I have finally arrived with my Teacher and am blessed with the motivation to stay plugged to Him—the giver of this precious jewel of silence. Instead of ending the online Kriya session, I silently exited the online room to stay in the '*Hall of Silence*' a little longer, dissolving into silent witness-hood. Later, when I opened my eyes and then my laptop, the first sentence I read was, "Listen to Him in deep silence." 😊

Note: When this story was posted on a local group, someone sent me the blog link where Mohanji had related this experience. The picture showed His hair, snowy white with vibhuti and was titled 'The Mount Kailash Effect'. In this story, I had compared it with Shiva and the snowy mountains without knowledge of this blog, the picture and the background story!

16 A technique from Mohanji's Empowered Series program.

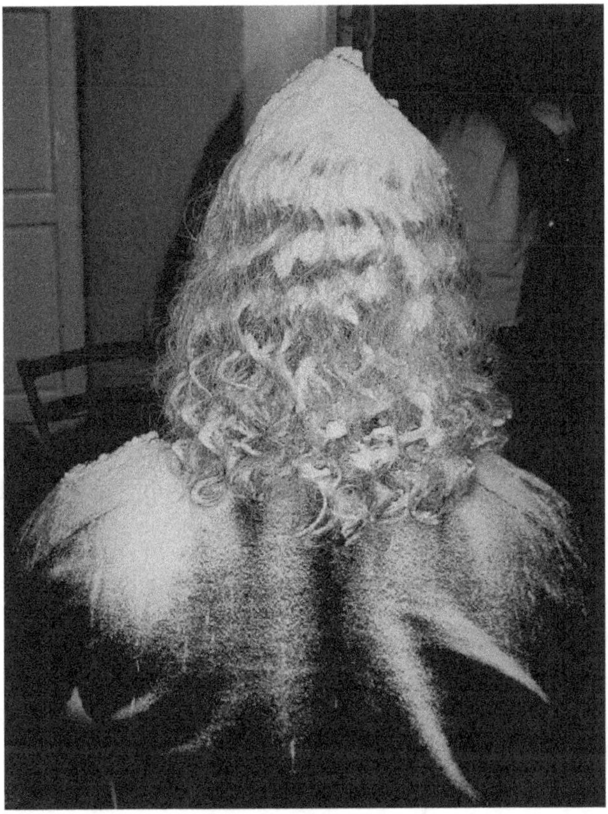

THE GURU PRINCIPLE

We are so blessed with Consciousness Kriya! We don't even realise how fortunate we are.

Having had a guru since 1991, I know how much we followers longed for physical contact with the Master (Swami). The *satsang* in the Master's presence was so benevolent, fulfilling, consoling and comforting that we could never have enough of it—like tasting sugar. Our Master abundantly blessed us to be in His presence for many years. Even though 'be like Me' and 'you and I are one' are His main teachings, we prefer to taste the sugar rather than become it.

However, we can experience oneness in silence with Consciousness Kriya. One morning I was struggling with thoughts again during the practice. I heard my inner Mohanji say, "*Guru Tattwa*". Somehow, I resonated with the words, even though unsure of the meaning. I suddenly found myself in deep silence, aware of my awareness and felt the immediate Presence of Mohanji as my inner awareness.

Later, when I looked up the phrase, I found that Guru Tattwa meant the Guru Principle. The term originates from Sanskrit—Guru means 'master' and tattwa means 'principle', 'essence', 'reality ' or 'truth'. The Guru can also be described as 'one who brings awareness', so Guru Tattwa is the essence of the One who brings awareness or higher knowledge.

This is deeper than the colours of life, for the colours are manifestations, whereas Guru is the Source of manifestation itself! Consciousness Kriya brings what Mohanji wants to bring to the world—Himself in His true form, the Essence of awareness, which is even deeper than awareness!

Jai Mohanji

ECSTASY

HAPPY KRIYA!

Blessed is the Kriya practice! What a gift of Consciousness. A gift from Mohanji.

It was difficult to focus during today's Consciousness Kriya practice, and I missed the inner connection. Then, the words, "*Happy Kriya!*" rose from deep inside. These words made me smile and helped me reconnect, accepting the temporary disturbances. I repeated the Kriya immediately after to focus better this time, then twenty-one Om recitations. I did! The focus was so razor-sharp that even my body resonated with the practice.

My spine started burning, and my hands and feet got warm. That was strange because I was sitting in an ice-cold room. Usually, I have ice-cold hands, even at seventeen degrees Celsius. My mind became a silent witness, melting in Mohanji's safe Presence. I was overwhelmed by a deep feeling of love, so profound that tears of joy flowed *inside* my body and being. I was watching the flow of existence in slow motion. After the Kriya practice, I could hardly utter my usual Ganesha chant or perform the paduka puja (ritual bathing of the Guru's feet). With every offering I made to the small silver padukas[17], I felt my existence, movements and offerings melting together in a

17 Metal or wooden slippers representing the feet of the Divine. In this case, the Guru's feet

blend of almost tangible ecstasy. How blessed are we to have Mohanji through Him, the access to a sacred, secret pathway to the inner realms of our existence!

Jai Mohanji! ♡♡♡

LEAVING ALREADY?

While doing Kriya practice, my mind drifted off. I heard Mohanji kindly say inside, "*Are you leaving already?*" I marvelled at His use of humour to articulate serious topics casually. When my monkey mind jumps up and down and drifts down memory lane or heads to Never Ever land, He is always there to get me back with tenderness, love and occasional humour.

I heard Him being strict with a core team member the other day, and she was taking it very graciously, knowing that He loves her tremendously and has no feelings of anger or ego. He corrects spot-on on the spot and then forgets straight away. Even my Master Swami, who passed away in 2020, was tremendously strict to His inner circle at times. After one of these scoldings, His boys told me that they needed it or else they would indeed become very tamasic. I felt lucky that Swami never chose to shout at me. Somehow, I guess he must have known that humour and love work more effectively on me.

AN EXPANSIVE LESSON

On 23rd January 2022 (Sunday), I asked Mohanji a question during the Empowerment 3.0 workshop about combining the practice of focusing on the spine with my mantra. Last year in August, Mohanji mentioned that focusing on the spine was one of the key practices during His days of *sadhana* (spiritual practice). I had incorporated it as a habit during my spare time, even while walking the dog outside. I first did the Pause technique to get aligned with my inner Mohanji and then focused on the spine, combining my breath with my Guru mantra for the rest of the walk. Even while driving, I did the same.

I told Mohanji about it and asked if it was fine. He encouraged me to keep doing it except while driving. I assumed that this general warning didn't apply to me. I was sure that I was experienced enough to handle it while driving. He may have mentioned it to warn other less 'advanced' people. Then, Tuesday arrived—the day that everything went wrong. We went on a short holiday to visit old friends from Limburg, a county in south Holland where we had lived for almost thirty years.

I had reasons to be upset that day. My husband was upset because our restaurant was closed due to the lockdown, and I was upset because this affected his behaviour towards me. This time, we didn't get any financial compensation. Further, the very thought of reopening the restaurant after the lockdown stressed him. How to get enough staff with everyone moving on to other jobs? The weather was gloomy. Worry made my husband's speech harsh, which hurt me. Even my body was disturbed. Despite my efforts, I couldn't do anything about the situation, inside or outside. I watched myself getting lost in mind talk, and emotions. At one point, I was angry, sad, restless and desperate. I did the pause technique, but I didn't *stop* to pause. Through all this, I was talking to Mohanji.

I was frantically looking for a satisfying holiday activity. I wanted to be in Zen mode on a fun holiday in perfect weather with an understanding and humourous husband. I knew that these expectations wouldn't help with accepting the situation. We finally decided that I would visit a friend, and he would stay back and rest. I wasn't listening to my tired body.

With all the disturbances, I filled the wrong fuel in my husband's car. I drove towards the highway, did the Pause technique to align myself, focused on the spine and repeated my mantra. After a few kilometres, the car sputtered and slowed down. I realised something was very wrong and wondered about the issue. Then I realised what I had done and quickly and nervously moved the car to the emergency lane and called roadside assistance.

With a blood condition that makes my blood clot below 4 degrees Celsius, I almost started to hyperventilate as I waited for the tow truck in the cold night, with cars racing past me. I witnessed my reaction and called out to Mohanji for help. I also made a few emergency calls to my husband and the friend that I was meeting. I performed the steady Pause technique breathing with full attention since I had nothing else to do while waiting. Then it struck me that this was the expensive 'listen-to-and-trust-your-guru-for-your-own-and-others-sake' lesson. I shouldn't have performed the technique while driving.

The Empowerment training taught me not to harbour guilt feelings, and the prayer to Mohanji and the Masters created a safe and open space in my mind. I could think clearly and find a solution despite the threatening temperature. I called some friends who were kind enough to get their car to pick up my husband and come to my rescue. They arrived after the tow truck had towed my car to a safe place. It took another couple of hours to get the vehicle repaired.

We had *satsang* and cookies in the comfort of my dear friends' heated car. One hundred and twenty euros for car repair, three hours lost, a disturbed evening for my friends, stress, and a lost opportunity to meet my other friend. I was the third person that evening that mistakenly filled the wrong fuel. But help was around at a moment's notice. The people who came to assist were too kind—the tow truck driver, the mechanic, my friends, and my husband. I got to be in Zen mode on an (unintended) fun holiday activity in perfect weather (courtesy of the heated car) with an understanding and humourous husband.

This episode taught me that we could witness a mistake without judgment. Why add judgment to the already bad consequences that follow the wrong action? Of course, recognising the lesson doesn't always mean that we have internalized the lesson. As I finished writing this experience, I remembered a similar incident long before I met Mohanji.

I had just learned a powerful healing technique that involved a lot of breathing. I practised it in the car while driving and sent energy to the world. The V-string broke, and I was alert enough to pull over. I dismissed the strong and direct reaction of the car as a coincidence. We, women, think we can do many things simultaneously. But it is time to focus.

A NON-CONFIRMATIVE STATE

This morning I made a firm decision to stay aware during my practices. I went into the core of my focus and connected to Mohanji's Presence. I remembered His inner instruction *to focus on awareness* and did just that. I saw myself meditating inside my heart's cave, surrounded by the energy of all the lineage Masters. Mohanji was sitting next to me. All the other Masters were present, but I couldn't see them individually. It was more silent than silent. I heard my inner voice, "*You are in a non-confirmative state.*"

The image disappeared when I concentrated on my practice, but the silence remained. After the practice, the silence was so profound that I thought that even my heart had stopped beating. When my practice ended, I found the meaning of 'non-confirmative' on the internet—"a failure or refusal to conform, as with established customs, attitudes, or ideas."

I thought, "This is precisely the attitude or the state of the Masters: their state is beyond established customs, attitudes and ideas!" 🙏🙏🙏

Jai Mohanji!

EXPECT MIRACLES

At times, my Parabrahma Mohanji reflects the words or behaviour of my Master Swami when he was still amongst us in his physical form.

One night in November 2018 in Mumbai, we were invited to a follower's residence and eagerly awaited Swami's arrival. We had formed a line in the house's driveway. When He arrived, the car's door opened right in front of me, and Swami saw me first. He smiled with delight, surprise and confirmation. He said, "Linda! You have come!?" Without telling Him, He must have known that the timing was crazy. We were in the midst of an incredible move—shifting houses, county and profession, all at once.

We were opening an Indian vegetarian/vegan restaurant in the centre of Alkmaar, an exciting prospect after thirty plus years in fashion development and sales. I was sure that my longing to meet Swami was pure and would be supported. We refurbished and furnished the restaurant. The opening was a few days away. We were waiting for the Indian chefs to arrive. I had booked an earlier flight, but the timing couldn't have been better since the trip coincided with our idle wait time! Undoubtedly, the Master's grace. Both my persistence and the Masters' miraculous timing made this memorial visit possible.

Something similar happened with Mohanji during our recent London trip. Parvati and I had decided to travel together and had booked tickets for the event. The plan was to arrive a couple of days before and depart a day after. Parvati then realised that she had a necessary, unavoidable appointment the morning after the event. We would have to pay for an event ticket, three corona tests, taxi fares, return flights, and probably a hotel for a one-day event, which was also accessible online. Further, flying back in the middle of the night after the event would undoubtedly have triggered my migraine.

I decided against joining Parvati and cancelled my event ticket. I longed to meet Mohanji and be in His presence, but my frail health did not permit it. However, the lovely UK Team members assured us that we would be accommodated in a follower's house and suggested to expect miracles. It was a fantastic suggestion. Why not? I did! Sometimes we have to be reminded of the things we already know. I told Mohanji inwardly that I would love to see Him again, without expectations. I simply opened my being to the possibility of a beautiful weekend where everything flowed smoothly and then let go. Seconds later, Parvati called to mention that she could travel the following afternoon!

I rebooked my event ticket, and we started searching for flights. I could hardly concentrate due to bad flu and made the booking a day after KLM cancelled refunds in case of a positive COVID test. If I tested positive before my flight, I would lose my money, and Parvati would have to travel by herself. Nothing could be done now, so we simply surrendered. Nothing untoward happened, and we reached London safely.

The house of our warm and welcoming hosts, Yamini and Vivek, was more like a mansion or estate. On arrival, we heard the exciting news that Mohanji was expected that very evening. The program schedule was still unknown. No one knew what to expect. Parvati and I didn't know if we were even allowed to participate in the event. But we were happy to share in the high energy frequency buzz of the entire household. We were thrilled when we heard we could join the program.

We waited at the entrance hall for Mohanji to arrive. He was first lovingly welcomed by Yamini with an aarati[18]. As He passed me by, Mohanji looked in my eyes and with the same loving look, half surprised and half confirming, that Swami had given me in Mumbai a few years earlier. Mohanji said: 'Linda, you have come!', proving once again that no boundaries exist for a Master of the Nath Tradition, anytime, anywhere.

I noticed that I was critical of my every word and action in London. Insecurity came up. I didn't make it worse by criticising my inner critic. I just watched it. In the morning meditation, I surrendered and relaxed through the physical tension and stress caused by my inner critic. I felt Mohanji consoling my inner child and simply let my head rest on His shoulder. I heard Him say kindly, "*Rise from love.*"

How simple, loving and pointed these words were? Isn't that what we should do? Be kind. Start building from a foundation of love because anything else would collapse in time. Self-love is the best starting point. When I let love in, I could raise my frequency instantly.

This reminded me of an inner message from Mohanji, "*I will give you so much love that you will forget everything else.*"

The following day, another surprise awaited us. We were invited to visit the Shri Ram Mandir in London. Mohanji offered gorgeous gifts and aarati to Shri Jagannath. As Parvati and I entered the dining hall for lunch, Mohanji was coming

18 Waving lamps in front of a deity, Master or revered person to honour them

out of the hall. We presumed that He had blessed the food and would eat in a quiet room. We took our plates and searched for a place to sit. There was only a big table which had some empty spaces left. As we took our seats, Mohanji stepped into the hall and sat in front of me. We immediately took our plates and stood up to make room for his team and other group members. Mohanji smiled and motioned us to stay seated. We dropped back in our seats and were flabbergasted. I didn't know what to say or do, so I focused on conscious eating to let Mohanji eat in peace. With Mohanji sitting so close to us, it was a memorable practice.

I recalled a similar setting in a recent dream where I was casually sitting at a long dining table with Mohanji by my side, eating in silence. Ever since, I offer part of my food to Mohanji as if He is sitting at the table, as a reminder to eat more consciously since my body is very sensitive and can't digest everything I like to eat.

After lunch, I mentioned the dream to Mohanji. Pat came the reply with a smile, "It was not a dream!". I was in awe. How many unexpected blessings can one digest?

The next day, we attended the event at the Kensington Hotel in London. Mohanji graciously consented to individual and group pictures with everyone present. We waited our turn for the picture after the UK team, event participants, and the Skanda Vale Swamis and Sisters. Parvati saw Mohanji standing quite straight and not touching anyone. She smiled mischievously and said: 'We are not going to let Him get away with this, aren't we?' 'No. We will nicely snuggle up.", I responded. We giggled like small children, which we were. Our inner child still needs healing.

When we approached Mohanji, He immediately opened

His arms and wrapped His left arm around me. I naturally let my head rest on His shoulder, feeling loved and safe, just as in the meditation. The previous inner guidance, "*Rise from love*", became tangible. Somebody said that day, "Mohanji fulfils everyone's deepest desires." So true! I would add, "He fulfils more than one can even think. Better to stop thinking and enjoy in awe and gratitude." ♡

I DO!

After my Kriya practice, my whole being opened deeply and widely In the silence of Mohanji-nothingness. I heard Him say, "*I do*", which sounded like a wedding vow.

My memories rewinded thirty years to a dream where Krishna appeared in a bar. Despite this odd setting, I experienced Divine bliss. At that time, I was doing intense sadhana and thinking of God all the time. I had no other desire but to be with God at all times. I asked Krishna spontaneously to marry me. He answered, "*I cannot marry you, but I can elevate you (spiritually).*" Saying thus, he lifted me with Divine willpower. Literally, with bar stool and all, and without any physical contact!

I was floating with my energy elevated to higher levels. Back then, I didn't know anything about energy levels. Further, no one around me ever mentioned the concept of energy frequencies and the importance of raising one's frequency to higher levels. I still remember the uplifting feeling. After the dream, I had feelings of rejection, "Why could Krishna not marry me?" The thoughts of a twenty-seven-year-old girl!

Now, Krishna appeared in the form of Mohanji and said, "*I do*". Not to a person but Silence. Since I experienced the silence, there was this feeling of melting in oneness—no-one to connect to an-other. Silence married silence. No boundaries. No you and me. Only completion and fullness in nothingness.

A question arose, "What about Creation? I wasn't expecting

an answer, but one came from beyond my thinking mind, "*The Light is expressing itself as a soulmate.*" What profound beauty is in these simple words? I couldn't stop myself from sharing this experience. Silence is whole and complete in itself. It doesn't need anything to complement it. From that Wholeness, Creation happens through light. Thus, Silence and Creation are Soulmates.

I was a bit afraid of overloading readers with my experiences. Once during lunch in London, I asked Mohanji about this fear. And if I should stop sharing. He said, "You do it for yourself, right? Keep sharing. Some may get inspired. No one is forced to read it."

Jai Mohanji ♡♡♡

CROSS THE ROAD TO ETERNAL SILENCE

This morning during Kriya, I had a short inner conversation with Mohanji instead of concentrating on the practice 😉. I asked, "I seem to have lost the deep connection that I felt initially. What do I do?"

I then realised I had forgotten the impact of an earlier important communication a few weeks ago. "*I am the Father of Fathers.*"

In Hinduism, God as the Divine Masculine refers to the Eternal Silence or 'That', the Absolute or Parabrahma, which is the Source of all Creation (the Divine Feminine) and permeates all Creation.

I suddenly realised that I still regarded Mohanji as my *bada bhai* (big brother) even though He had revealed Himself as the eternal Father. My relationship, though intimate, restricted my perception of His power and all-pervasiveness. While my private conversations with Him as a sister made me feel safe and loved, it didn't do justice to Mohanji's stature—who He is and what He represents.

Addressing Him as the Father of Fathers restored my connection and elevated my energy to higher states. Then the thought arose, "The Kriya practice processes Kundalini (the Divine Feminine). How do I utilize the knowledge of connecting to Mohanji's energy as Parabrahma during Kriya?"

I got a flash of a Mohanji quote from the previous week

related to Silence (paraphrased from memory), "Imagine a busy road and a lovely couch on the other side. Now, keep your focus on being seated with your Master calmly and quietly on that couch. Over time, there will be only Silence (Divine Masculine), no matter how many cars (Creation or Divine Feminine) pass.

I realised that Consciousness Kriya is similarly a means to safely cross the busy road of the mind to the Eternal Silence within through awareness. Not by blocking the traffic by throwing oneself in front of the incoming cars of thoughts, words and actions but by being a silent witness on the couch (our Parabrahma) and watching the noise and movements until the Silence (Parabrahma) pervades everything.

NATH YOGIS

Both Mohanji and Swami are from the Nath Tradition[19]—a rich lineage of Masters connected with infinite consciousness, starting with Shiva and his consort Parvati (Adinath and Umanath in the Tradition). It continues with the Nav Nath (the nine Nath) Masters, the legendary Matysendranath and Gorakshnath being the foremost among them. Shirdi Sai Baba also belongs to this glorious Tradition. There are various books about the Tradition, its history and its Masters.

Each Nath Master has his unique expression in the world—as with Mohanji and Swami. Swami's mission was on a small scale. Living and working from his two ashrams in Girinagar, Bangalore and Nidaghatta, Maddur, he spread his message to the world by simply setting an unparalleled example of Divine worship. In contrast, Mohanji reaches out globally as a philanthropist and humanitarian, dedicating every word and action to elevate collective consciousness beyond species through many registered organisations, global platforms and initiatives to add value to the world, transforming mankind into kind men.

In the last few years of his incarnation, we knew Swami by His monastic name, Swami Shri Sai Prabuddhananda Saraswati. In this manifestation, He adorned a new look by wearing kundals

---

19 You can read Mohanji's book, Mast—The Ecstatic for a detailed account of the Nath Tradition.

(earrings) as per the Nath Tradition. I and many others have seen Mohanji in different embodiments of Divinity, resembling Shiva, Jesus, etc.

Both are Dattavadhootas[20] who take an Avatar to reform their followers to release them from the birth and death cycle. Swami explained His connection with these Avatars, 'We are glittering and glowing bulbs dangling along a single wire showing light to the world from our respective spaces, powered by the same current flowing through the wire.'

Mohanji explains, "There have been numerous Datta Avatars (incarnates). A Datta Avatar has raised themself to or come with the operating frequency of Lord Dattatreya. Datta is the state where three hundred and thirty million dimensions are projected from the one Source. The whole universe is the projection of that one Source—pure bright Consciousness.

When there are no fears and frames, what remains is Datta! **Datta is Love.** Unconditional Love! Not the usual transactional love with its in-built, hidden expectations. It doesn't matter who you are; our connection is love without expectations. Just love unconditionally.

20 Datta is a short form for Lord Dattatreya, a unique incarnation of the Divine Trinity—Brahma, Vishnu and Shiva. Avadhootas are Masters who have attained liberation and exist in complete freedom. You can read Mohanji's book, Mast—The Ecstatic to know more about Avadhootas

MORE INNER GUIDANCE AND DIRECTIONS

- *Let me do the work*
- *Stay focused*
- *Let me do the thinking*
- *Kriya is your lifeline to God realisation*
- *Just because I am no-nonsense doesn't mean I am hard*
- *Life is like a beautiful flower. Enjoy the fragrance*
- *Stay plugged in, and you will feel open and pure*
- *Keep moving from spirit to soul*
- *Soul is awareness*
- *The silence of forever*
- *Resistance is the leak (through which energy dissipates)*
- *Cut through the clutter (with your concentration and awareness)*
- *Be like a laser*
- *Let all the hearts exchange*
- *Do positive actions*
- *I can continue to love you further*
- *Be omnipresent (instead of focusing on fear)*
- *Maintain inner purity*
- *Don't use the energy. Be the energy!*
- *Enter this hall of silence. This is my gift for you.*

www.ingramcontent.com/pod-product-compliance
Lightning Source LLC
Chambersburg PA
CBHW062202160726
48282CB00027B/959
* 9 7 8 9 3 9 4 6 4 2 0 2 7 *